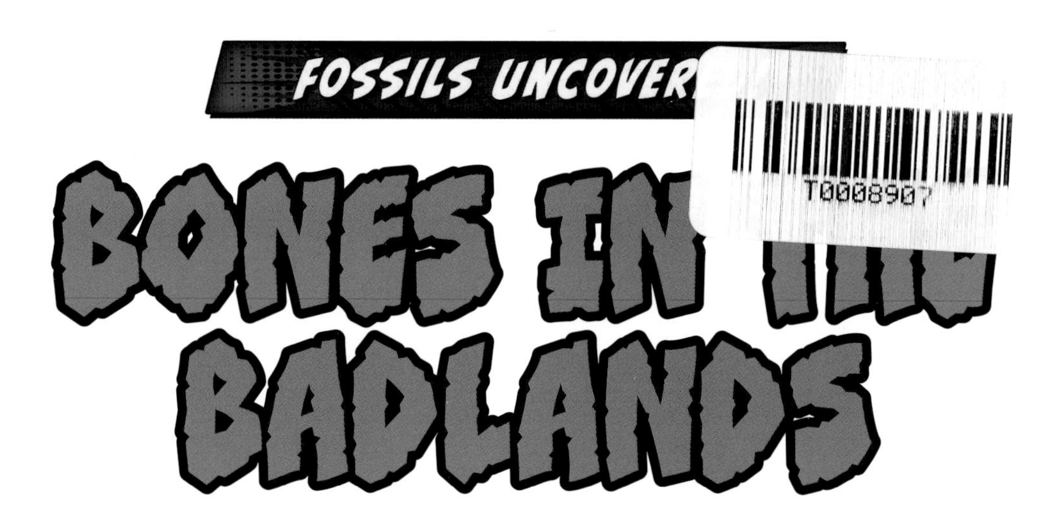

ALBERTOSAURUS DISCOVERY

By Sarah Eason
Illustrated by Diego Vaisberg

Minneapolis, Minnesota

Credits: 20b, © Catmando/Shutterstock; 21t, © Elenarts/Shutterstock; 21b, © Nobu Tamura/Wikimedia Commons; 22l, © Kriengsak Wiriyakrieng/Shutterstock; 22r, © Microgen/Shutterstock; 23b, © LegART/Shutterstock.

Editor: Jennifer Sanderson
Proofreader: Harriet McGregor
Designer: Paul Myerscough
Picture Researcher: Rachel Blount

DISCLAIMER: This graphic story is a dramatization based on true events. It is intended to give the reader a sense of the narrative rather than a presentation of actual details as they occurred.

Library of Congress Cataloging-in-Publication Data

Names: Eason, Sarah, author. | Vaisberg, Diego, 1981- illustrator.
Title: Bones in the badlands : albertosaurus discovery / by Sarah Eason ; illustrated by Diego Vaisberg.
Description: Bear claw books. | Minneapolis, Minnesota : Bearport Publishing Company, [2022] | Series: Fossils uncovered! | Includes bibliographical references and index.
Identifiers: LCCN 2021026712 (print) | LCCN 2021026713 (ebook) | ISBN 9781636913346 (library binding) | ISBN 9781636913414 (paperback) | ISBN 9781636913483 (ebook)
Subjects: LCSH: Currie, Philip J.--Juvenile literature. | Albertosaurus--Canada, Western--Juvenile literature. | Albertosaurus--Canada, Western--Comic books, strips, etc. | Dinosaur tracks--Canada, Western--Juvenile literature. | Paleontological excavations--Canada, Western--Juvenile literature. | Paleontology--Cretaceous--Juvenile literature. | Badlands--Canada, Western--Juvenile literature.
Classification: LCC QE862.S3 E273 2022 (print) | LCC QE862.S3 (ebook) | DDC 567.912--dc23
LC record available at https://lccn.loc.gov/2021026712
LC ebook record available at https://lccn.loc.gov/2021026713

For more information, write to Bearport Publishing, 5357 Penn Avenue South, Minneapolis, MN 55419. Printed in the United States of America.

CONTENTS

CHAPTER 1

A BASEMENT DISCOVERY

In 1996, **paleontologist** Philip Currie was searching for clues in the basement of the American Museum of Natural History. He wanted to learn how dinosaurs had lived.

Most scientists at the time thought that meat-eating dinosaurs had lived alone.

Philip wasn't so sure. He knew that fossil hunter Barnum Brown had found a group of bones together in the early 1900s.
IT MAY BE POSSIBLE THAT THESE ANIMALS LIVED AND HUNTED IN PACKS, LIKE SOME **CARNIVORES** DO TODAY. IF ONLY I COULD FIND PROOF.

Then, Philip made an amazing discovery.
THESE ARE ALBERTOSAURUS* BONES. COULD THESE BE...?
*al-bur-toh-SOR-uhss

Philip shared his finding with a fellow paleontologist.
LOOK AT ALL THESE BONES. THEY'RE ALL FROM THE BADLANDS OF WESTERN CANADA.
AND YOU THINK THEY ARE FROM AT LEAST NINE DIFFERENT ANIMALS?

YES—AND THAT'S NOT ALL. LOOK WHAT ELSE I'VE FOUND.
FIELD NOTES... AND A PHOTO OF A DIG SITE.
THESE ARE BARNUM BROWN'S NOTES! THAT MUST MEAN THESE BONES ARE THE ONES HE FOUND.
BARNUM'S NOTES SAY HE BROUGHT BACK ONLY SOME BONES FROM EACH ANIMAL. THERE MUST BE MORE.
THEN LET'S GO FIND THE REST!
Philip was excited by what this new discovery might mean.

CHAPTER 2

PHILIP'S QUESTIONS

And some **predators** also live in groups. They need to stay together to hunt for food.

Scientists know that some plant-eating dinosaurs lived in groups.
FACING A GROUP ALONE WOULD MAKE IT DIFFICULT FOR A SINGLE MEAT-EATER OF THE PAST TO HUNT, JUST LIKE IT DOES FOR PREDATORS OF TODAY...
...BUT IT WOULD BE MUCH EASIER FOR A GROUP. MAYBE ALBERTOSAURS LIVED—AND HUNTED—TOGETHER!

ROAAAR!
ROAAAR!

CHAPTER 3

SEARCHING IN THE BADLANDS

Philip brought a team to Canada, where the group got to work right away.

But finding the bones wasn't easy. Barnum hadn't made a map or written down where he had found the fossils.

Still, Philip searched on.

And soon...

Philip raced to the others to share the news.

For months, the team carefully dug up fossils.

WE'RE ONE STEP CLOSER TO KNOWING MORE ABOUT THESE DINOSAURS.

CHAPTER 4

LEARNING MORE

COULD THIS HAVE BEEN A PLACE WHERE THEY BUILT NESTS?
IF THEY HAD GATHERED TO LAY EGGS, THE ANIMALS WOULD ALL BE ABOUT THE SAME AGE.
BUT WE FOUND SKELETONS OF YOUNG ANIMALS AS WELL AS OLD ANIMALS.
BUT WE STILL NEED MORE **EVIDENCE** TO PROVE THAT MEAT-EATERS LIVED TOGETHER...

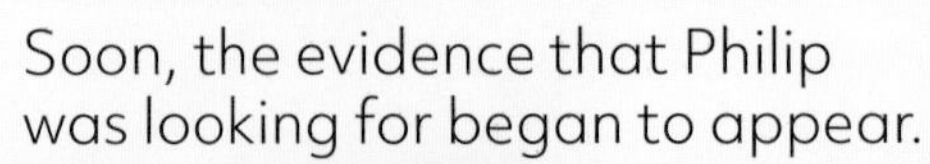
Soon, the evidence that Philip
was looking for began to appear.

HEY, PHILIP, IT'S RODOLFO CORIA. I'M IN ARGENTINA...

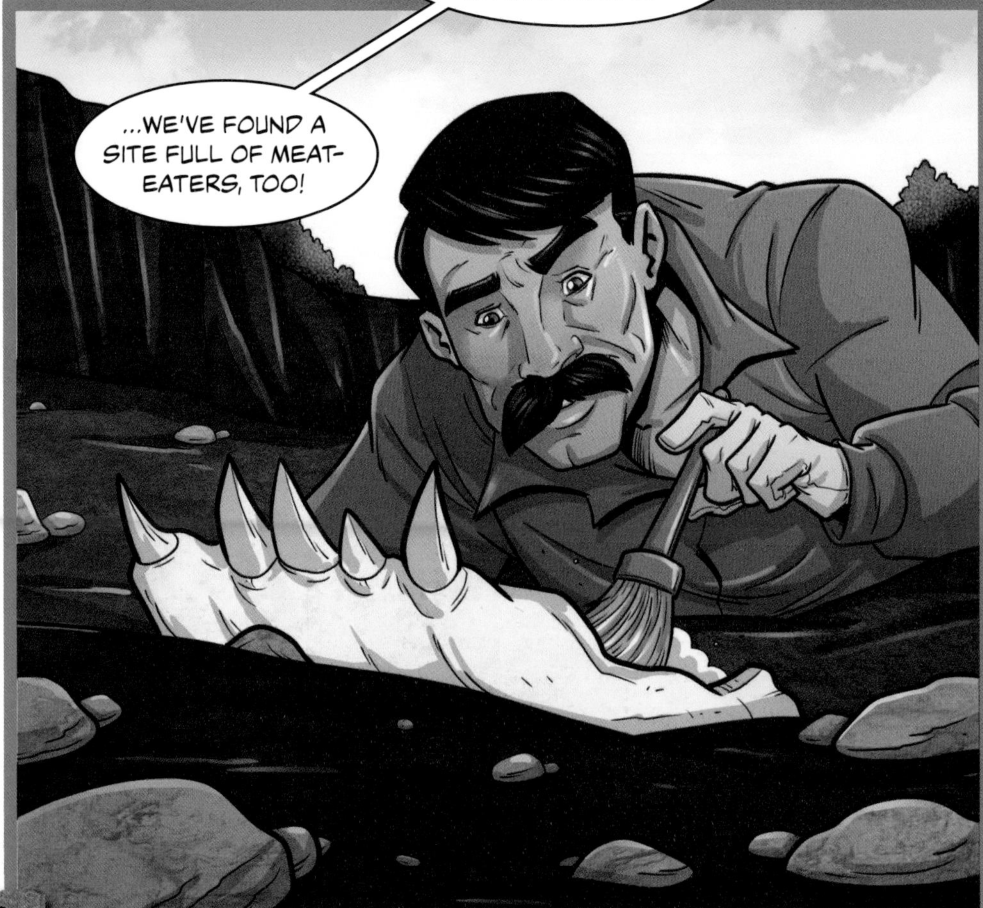
...WE'VE FOUND A SITE FULL OF MEAT-EATERS, TOO!

The presence of more than one site helped prove Philip's **theory** that meat-eaters had lived together. Soon, other paleontologists also made similar discoveries around the world.

Philip also found the footprints of a group of meat-eaters.

The bones in the badlands showed that there is much more to meat-eaters like *Albertosaurus* than was once thought. And as long as there are fossils to be found, paleontologists like Philip will keep digging them up and telling their stories!

Who Lived with *Albertosaurus*?

Dinosaurs lived on Earth for around 150 million years. Scientists divide the time in which the dinosaurs lived into three periods—the Triassic period (252 to 201 million years ago), the Jurassic period (201 to 145 million years ago), and the Cretaceous period (145 to 66 million years ago).

Albertosaurus lived about 70 million years ago, during the Cretaceous period. Here are three prehistoric animals that lived at the same time as *Albertosaurus*.

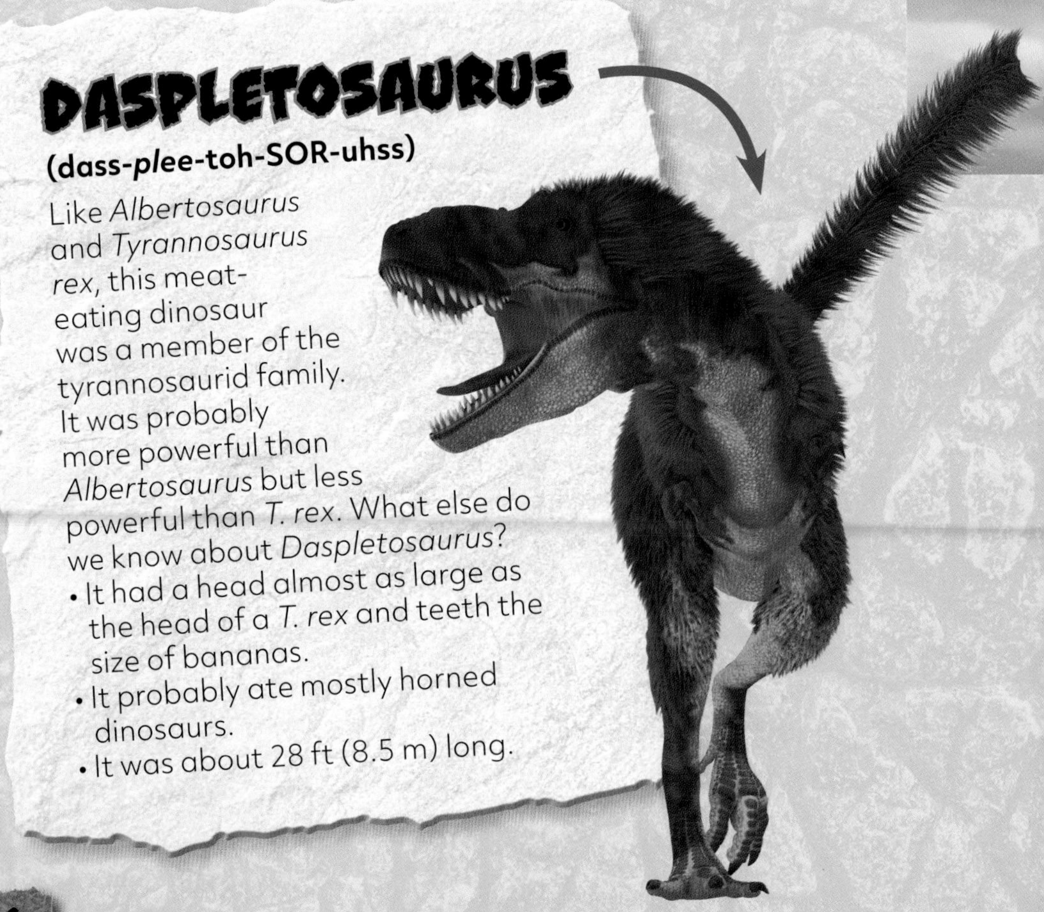

DASPLETOSAURUS

(dass-*plee*-toh-SOR-uhss)

Like *Albertosaurus* and *Tyrannosaurus rex*, this meat-eating dinosaur was a member of the tyrannosaurid family. It was probably more powerful than *Albertosaurus* but less powerful than *T. rex*. What else do we know about *Daspletosaurus*?

- It had a head almost as large as the head of a *T. rex* and teeth the size of bananas.
- It probably ate mostly horned dinosaurs.
- It was about 28 ft (8.5 m) long.

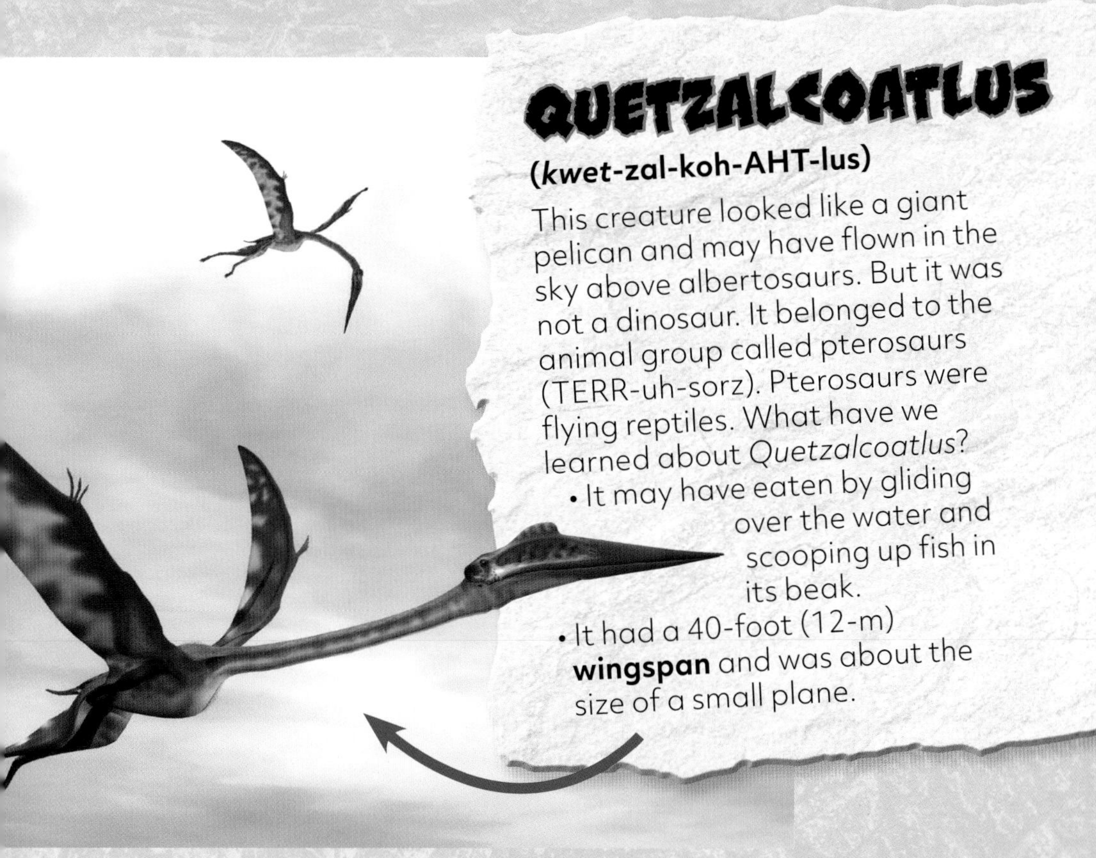

QUETZALCOATLUS

(*kwet*-zal-koh-AHT-lus)

This creature looked like a giant pelican and may have flown in the sky above albertosaurs. But it was not a dinosaur. It belonged to the animal group called pterosaurs (TERR-uh-sorz). Pterosaurs were flying reptiles. What have we learned about *Quetzalcoatlus*?

- It may have eaten by gliding over the water and scooping up fish in its beak.
- It had a 40-foot (12-m) **wingspan** and was about the size of a small plane.

HYPACROSAURUS **(hye-*pak*-ruh-SOR-uhss)**

Hypacrosaurus was first found by Barnum Brown in Alberta, Canada. This plant-eating dinosaur may have been eaten by *Albertosaurus*. Discover more about this potential prey.

- It had a mouth shaped like a duck's bill and a body part called a crest on top of its head.
- It probably came together in groups for at least part of the year.
- It had a call that may have sounded like a deep trumpet.
- It was about 30 ft (9 m) long.

What Is Paleontology?

Paleontology is the study of fossils, which are what is left of things that lived millions of years ago. Fossils are found in rock. Paleontologists use special tools to carefully remove the fossils from the rock so they can study them. By studying fossils, paleontologists can figure out where a plant or animal lived, what it looked like, and how it lived.

SOMETIMES PALEONTOLOGISTS STUDY FOSSILS IN LABS. THERE, THEY CAN USE MORE TOOLS TO LEARN ABOUT ANCIENT PLANTS AND ANIMALS.

Fossils can show how living things changed over time, too. Paleontologists can use fossils to find out what happened to an **environment** in the past and how living things **adapted** to the changes.

WHILE WORKING IN THE FIELD, PALEONTOLOGISTS OFTEN USE A SPECIAL BRUSH TO REMOVE LOOSE PIECES OF ROCK AND DUST FROM FOSSILS.

Glossary

adapted changed in order to handle new conditions

badlands a remote region with rocks that have been made into unusual shapes by strong wind and rain

carnivores animals that eat meat

dig site the place at which paleontologists have been digging for fossils

environment the conditions that surround a living thing

evidence proof of something

field notes information that a scientist writes down while working and exploring at a site

fossils the hardened remains of things that lived long ago

paleontologist a scientist who studies fossils to find out about life in the past

predators animals that hunt and eat other animals

prey animals that are hunted and eaten by other animals

quicksand wet sand into which heavy objects can sink

theory an idea that explains something

wingspan the measurement of a bird's wings from the tip of one wing to the tip of the other

FOSSILS HELP SCIENTISTS UNDERSTAND WHAT DINOSAURS LOOKED LIKE. THEY CAN USE THIS INFORMATION TO BUILD MODELS OF THEM.

Index

Read More

Clay, Kathryn. *Albertosaurus (Smithsonian Little Explorer. Little Paleontologist)*. North Mankato, MN: Capstone Press, 2019.

Gregory, Joy. *Paleontologist (STEM Careers)*. New York: AV2 by Weigl, 2020.

Woodward, John. *Dinosaur! Dinosaurs and Other Amazing Prehistoric Creatures as You've Never Seen Them Before*. New York: DK Publishing, 2019.

Learn More Online

1. Go to **www.factsurfer.com** or scan the QR code below.
2. Enter "**Bones Badlands**" into the search box.
3. Click on the cover of this book to see a list of websites.